50/50

By: Tinina Robinson & Tyra Robinson

CreateSpace Independent Publishing Platform, North Charleston, SC
Robinson, Tinina
50/50

LCCN: 2017918350
ISBN-13: 978-1533140272
ISBN-10: 1533140278

ACKNOWLEDGMENTS

To who has opened my heart, my baby girl Tyra. I've never wanted to complete something so bad to watch you shine. I know that everything hasn't fell right into place of how you want it, but I think it's only happening slower for you to recognize all your other talents. You are my best part of life along with your sister and brother. You've changed who I am stealing my heart when I had you. We've been inseparable since. Just like air I need you, you're my Gemini twin. I want you to know that I'm honored to have written a book with you. It's so amazing to me to have watched you learn how to talk to talk with me, to learn how to walk and walk with me…to learn how to write and write with me. I love everything about you and thank you for giving me a life to live for.

To who has made my heart bigger to love another, my daughter Asia. Thank you for being there through all moods. You're always so willing to sit, listen and really hear. You put that blunt honesty in there which I look at as caring about the outlook. I love everything about you my baby but most of all how much you love me.

To the person who filled and closed my heart to just love all who's in it, my son Sabean. You're my last baby now young man. The joy I feel watching you achieve the things that you want is unexplainable. I always tell you that we came in this together because I had you, but you were strong for me. Nothing can take away that need for each other. I love you with every breath in me.

Poem/Poetry Index

Dedication Page

An author named me
I came into the world knowing nothing
Blank pages you filled, you gave me life
My first pages are written with all your memories
I took in everything you said to me
You heard my first words
You showed me how to write sentences
Every sentence started with a capital letter and every
sentence ended with a period
I got to share a couple of years with you before you added
chapters to your book
Chapter 2 and Chapter 3
Another girl and a little boy
Our stories became greater in detail because of those two
We gave you a never ending story
Your whole world was complete
I want to personally thank you
Every chapter I have is because of you
I'm living a story I would never have if I didn't have you
You know almost every page in my book
You helped me turn pages I would've just ripped out
With you I'm an open book
I love the non-fiction side of you
You're my favorite book
I read you everyday
I grew up learning you and you grew older teaching me
You are an inspiration to me

I wish more people can see the way you write...your
talented ways
I love you so much
I dedicated this page of my story to you

By: Tyra Robinson

Abracadabra

You appeared when I wasn't looking
You shuffled with my emotions enough to make me think
I was your Queen
You unlocked my heart without me giving you a key
Everything was happening so fast, you seemed so perfect
to me
I would see things with my own eyes that made me think
differently, but when confronted
you would say sorry for all the wrongs you did to me
That would always fix anything; it never made sense to me
You had to have messed with my mind to make me believe
everything you said to me
Your lies became truths when you whispered in my
ear…you told me what you thought I wanted to hear
I would always be mad about your disappearing acts, but
you would always come back
You knew when and how to use your special wand…that
was part of the reason I would always take you back
It was like you had control over me but not of me
I only stayed because you created an illusion that you
really loved me
You performed all your tricks right in front of me
I fell in love with you…how couldn't I?
You got me to believe in magic

By: Tyra Robinson

Silently Speaking

A stranger that I once was in love with was now standing
next to me but with someone else
I wish I was in this elevator by myself or just with you
I haven't seen you in so long, but I couldn't bring myself to
say hi to you
I was going through so many emotions in that moment
Happy to see that you're doing ok
Sad that you were once mine and you aren't anymore
Mad that I see the girl who took my place
I looked at you for a good five seconds because I didn't
know if I would ever run into you again
A glimpse of you brought my mind down memory lane
It made me travel to a place we'll never be at again
In love I was again…with our memories
We had so much history
The silence in the elevator was killing me
I miss you even though you're standing so close to me
The elevator reached your floor and I let you go
No hi or goodbye
My past just looked back and smiled before the doors
closed
I was back alone in reality

By: Tyra Robinson

Dear Wrong One,

I'm sorry
This whole thing started accidentally
He was just a friend to me
He got out of the friend zone because of all you did to me
You lied and he would tell the truth
You cheated and even though he and I aren't together he
is faithful to me
You hurt me and he would make everything better
You loved me, but he has always been in love with me
I'm in love with that now
He shows me what I deserve
He brings out the best in me
I'm trying to be happy with you, but he makes me happy
I'm ready to change our situation for him
He's giving me something you never will
You won't ever be the man I want you to be
I don't want to lose something I've always had
Thank you for pushing me into the arms of someone who's
ready to hold me
He's everything you could never be
P.S. I'm realizing now I should've left a long time ago

By: Tyra Robinson

Where Am I?

I forgot what I look like
When I look in the mirror I see someone who resembles
the person I used to be
My reflection shows someone who I never thought I
would be
I live in a body that doesn't fit me
I used to be fun and go out but now I'm a homebody
I used to love to shop until I noticed that the cute clothes
that I want don't fit me
I used to get attention because of my cute figure and
personality... now guys don't even try to talk to me
I'm not confident anymore
Fat doesn't look good on me
I'm trapped beneath a layer of insecurity
I gained weight and lost sight of me
I'm trying to find myself
My own body is hiding me
I disappeared and nobody else is searching for me because
they accepted what they now see
I'll never get used to this extra person of me
I'm missing my life living this way and I'll never be ok
until the current me shapes into a picture of my past
I'm ready to appear in the mirror again
I miss the old me

By: Tyra Robinson

Broadcast

A "loyal" person can't always be considered trustworthy
Don't be surprised when your business comes out
It's public information once you share it with someone else
That someone just runs and tells somebody else
They can't keep it to themselves
You just gave away breaking news, of course they run and
tell somebody else
"She told me" That's how it always starts out
It's not just females who run their mouth
A guy will when he's trying to prove a point
He just won't share his gossip until he has to
If not right away it's just stored away in their mind
All it takes is that someone or somebody to get mad
enough to air all your dirt out
They use it against you because you gave them something
to tell
Hurt always comes out the same
You just have to know that you're taking a risk letting
someone know the unknown about you
Don't tell all your business to someone who has a mouth
Don't tell all your business to someone who just sits there
and listens
I think that's really anybody and everybody so honestly be
careful who you speak to
They Talk

By: Tyra Robinson

Somewhere Else

It's easy to say goodbye when you didn't get a chance to
say it
There would have been no other way I would've been able
to accept it
Today I lost you, but I know where you are
You traveled to a place called heaven, it's somewhere
beyond the stars
I've never been there, but I've been told it's where all the
angels are
So if it's anything like I've imagined
In the day you hide behind clouds and in the night you
become a star
Life is neither near nor far
If I keep remembering then your life will stay right here
on earth
Goodbye is a word only said when you're leaving but
you're gone
You're in a better place (R)esting (I)nside (P)rayers
You were given life then it was taken away, but we are all
here to live once
Nobody will stay
So I know that I will see you again someday

By: Tyra Robinson

Liar, Liar

Don't be naïve
A guy will tell you anything
"I'll stop talking to her"
That's a lie
If he was able to talk to her without you knowing why
would he stop just because you found out?
He'll find another way for them to stay in touch
Another lie
"She's just a friend"
If you never seen her and he has never mentioned her
before then she's not just a friend
She's just a friend with benefits
Another lie
"My phone died"
Has his phone ever died before? He turned his phone off
because he was occupied with somebody else
Another lie
"I was out with my friends"
If he doesn't pick up the phone when you call when he
was out with his "friends" and the next day he tells you
that he was out with them, then he was out acting like a
single man
Another lie
"I promise"
If he ever tells you that that means it will never happen
He's thinking you'll forget and he most likely has forgotten
Another lie

"I didn't fuck her"
If you have to ask him "did you fuck her?" expect him to answer with another lie
Why would he just say yes? He'll say no because he still wants to fuck you
Another lie
"I don't know her"
If she's in his phone he knows her
The only way you probably know about her is because he knows her and you're just finding out about her
Another lie
"I love you"
That's something that becomes a lie
If he ever hurt you did he ever really love you?
If it's something he tells you too early before he even knows it's true, it's just to sleep with you
A man will tell you a book of lies and title it Truth
He goes along with the story as long as you do
As long as you're on the same page he can add to the story as much as he wants to
You're still listening

By: Tyra Robinson

Princess

Your money pulled me in
Your personality kept me around
You loved my beauty and I loved a beast
The rose died when you put your hands on me
The way you loved me was scary
You didn't want to lose me so you gave me what I wanted
You showed me a life I would never have without you
I lived in a castle that I was locked in as long as I abided by
all your rules
Not only were you taking care of me but you were taking
care of my family too
You had control of me mentally and physically
I couldn't mess up the life my family was now used to
I couldn't leave because I was too afraid of you
I don't know when you changed me
I was never scared of leaving a man that I dealt with, but
you became too obsessed with me
I couldn't be anywhere without you
I was your trophy and you didn't want anyone thinking
they could have me
I couldn't talk to anyone without you being there listening
You had to know what I was saying and who I was saying
things to
You were making me believe that the way you was
treating me was ok because I could do anything I wanted
as long as it was done with you
You let me have freedom to an extent

I would do whatever you wanted because your anger
would leave marks on me
Bruises that nobody else would see
Everybody was free
I gave up my freedom to stay with who loved me

By: Tyra Robinson

"I Don't"

I am your wife
How could you do this to me?
We've been married for ten years, but the last five years I
guess our vows didn't mean anything
You had another relationship like I died and you was
starting all over again
Not only did I just find out about her but I now found out
she's having your baby
We don't even have kids
You told me you didn't want kids, but now you want me
to accept the one you're having with someone else
You're telling me you want to work things out
You're telling me that I'm the only woman that matters to
you
You're telling me you don't love her
I don't know what you've been telling her
You're apologizing to me thinking that I'm going to just be
fine with everything you did
This is a mistake you can't erase
I'll never be ok with sitting around a reminder of what you
did to me
I won't love a child that's not mine and I'll never be ok
with you having to co-parent
My husband is now going to be somebody's father
She gave you a title I would've been ok with giving you
You're my husband
You stepped out on me

I thought we were happy
I don't know how you expect me to ever trust you again
She'll get to see a side of you I always wanted to
She'll get to have the only person my heart has ever loved
because you ruined what we had
I have to learn to live without what I thought was my
future
You have to learn to live without me, but you have a little
family now
I allowed us to try to be how we used to be the last three
months of her pregnancy
I wanted to see if it really was your baby
She looked just like you
Divorce was necessary
I couldn't stay committed to someone I didn't marry
I lived the best years of my life with you and separation
was now all I asked of you

By: Tyra Robinson

He never took it off

Dumb bitch
When your wife asked me if I messed with you I
responded with "I do"
"I do fuck him on his business trips"
"I do take care of him when he's sick"
"I do love him"
I told you if she ever found out about me then I would tell
her the truth, the whole truth and nothing but the truth
I could provide her with plenty of proof
I told her you came onto me
I told her I asked about your wedding ring I seen
I told her you told me that you was married, but you
wasn't that happy
I backed off after that, but you kept contacting me
I became a friend, but your consistency and interest in me
slowly had me thinking what this could be
You talked me into seeing you again and after that we
started hanging out
Then we started going on dates and getting to know each
other
I was dating a married man
Things with us seemed so content
I was making you happy
So happy that you told me you would leave your wife for
me

I believed you because you were acting like a divorce is
something you had been thinking about since you started
messing around with me
It's probably been a good two years now of you telling me
this lie
Now that I had your wife actually texting me I told her
that you said you would be leaving her for me
After that she stopped texting me and you showed up at
my house about an hour later to end it with me
You was mad because I actually talked to your wife and
now she knew about us
You straight out just told me this was over
You loved your wife
You were never leaving her and then you just left
That was the last time I heard from you
You didn't try to write me
You didn't try to see me and you changed your number
I guess you were trying to save your marriage that "I"
almost ruined
The thing is you started this whole thing, but I'm a dumb
bitch for thinking that a married man with his wedding
ring on when he met me was going to leave his wife

By: Tyra Robinson

Drunk

Do you want me to refresh your memory about what you
said to me?
You spoke it so flowingly, so naturally
I didn't know that's how you felt... about me
You expressed true feelings
Telling me things you couldn't while sober
Well those things you kept in came out
Speaking carelessly, not thinking about my feelings as you
blurted shit out
The more I talked the more thoughts I got out of you
You're apologizing now for your shots
You was drunk, but that doesn't excuse what was said
You can blame it on the alcohol, but you're the one who
was letting everything spill out
You wasn't choking when you spoke, so you can't take it
back
Telling me you're sorry, you don't even remember what
you said
You let your mind speak for the first time while feeling
nothing at all
That's what really hurt my feelings
That you said it out loud
I was talking to a different side of you...that didn't care
what I thought
I heard everything I needed to hear

By: Tyra Robinson

Can I do this again?

If I fell once why would I want to fall again?
I'm tired of hurting myself
Falling in love with the wrong man
It's not easy to get over a person
So why would I want to let another in
He made me fall so hard and never want to get up again
Trust again or love again
He left me with invisible scars
Bruised and broken within
You want to mend something that won't be fixed
completely again
I'm scared, I'm scared to let you...in
I don't know if I'm ready to get that close, to another man
New love brings new pain
And I just can't go through that again

By: Tyra Robinson

I'm tangled

I like you
I like you because you care about me
I like you because of how you say things to me
I like you because you know me
We've been friends for many years
One experience made feelings I never had appear
That night I thought you had seen me differently, but the
next day you looked at me the same
I was still just your "friend"
Days went by
Months passed
Those feelings of mine never left
Unfortunately they only grew because here and there we
would still be doing things friends shouldn't do
We slowly became friends with benefits
You were the only one benefiting from it
You were getting something you wanted without being in
a relationship
I was getting nothing but mixed feelings
I wanted something
I started seeing boyfriend qualities in the way you have
always treated me
I never wanted to mess up the bond we had so I would
never tell you that
I know you didn't want an actual relationship with me and
that's why we stayed friends
You told me about all your ex-girlfriends

You told me everything
I'm sure you would tell me if you wanted something more
with me
I had to learn to hide whatever I felt for you because I was
more scared of possibly losing you
Unraveling the truth, I didn't want to loosen us
I didn't want to untangle any strings
I was the one that was attached

By: Tyra Robinson

You're not interested enough

Are you interested in me?
I feel like I'm bothering you
I'm the only one starting up conversations
I understand that sometimes you're busy, but when you're
not you're not talking to me
Are you interested in me?
When we talk we have good long conversations
I'm expecting you to reach out to me the next day, but
when you don't it's like the conversation didn't mean
anything
Are you interested in me?
The things you say to me is making me
think that you are
You say you like me, but you don't care to hang out too
much
You say you want to get to know me, but you never ask
too many questions
Sometimes I think you're just talking to me
because I want to
It's not like you care to talk to me
Are you interested in me?
I feel like you don't think about me as much as I think
about you
You say you miss me just to make me think you do
You talk to me when you want to... just to let me know
you're around and to make me think that you care about
me more than you really do

Are you really interested in me?
You don't have to pretend to be
Pretending only gets me to grow real feelings
We don't need to communicate if you're not interested

By: Tyra Robinson

Say it, Do it

Stop falling in love with conversation just because he's
saying all the right things to you
He said those things to somebody else and he's just
repeating it to you
He's really just good at conversating
You're hearing it for the first time, but it's really nothing
new
He will say things to you and not even mean it while the
feelings are growing for you
He's just saying enough to "get" something out of the
conversation
He's not taking anything away from it
He's just learning how much he needs to say to you to
make you feel a certain way for him
Once he has you thinking that he cares, thinking that he
loves you words like "I love you" will have no real
meaning for him
He didn't have to show you
He just had to speak in a believable way after paying
enough attention to you
There were no actions behind what he was saying
His words were enough for you
You showed him that he didn't have to work to get you
Just speak it into existence and it would be reality for you
Men like him don't know how to treat a woman the right
way and so they treat every woman the same way

Women like you won't keep a man because you don't
change the behavior of this type of man
Speak to them in a way that nobody has before
Make them want more than a conversation
Actions speak louder than words
You'll be falling in love with what he's actually doing
instead of hearing him say it

By: Tyra Robinson

He Must

A man who loves me will need to get down on one knee
and ask to marry me
I would never ever get down on my knee to propose to
him
I'm not forcing him into a forever
When he's ready to pop the question, he will ask
I rather wait around a lifetime for him to ask rather than
marry someone who wasn't even thinking about that
He has to want it
He has to be willing to be even more committed to a legal
commitment
He has to realize that I'm all he has ever wanted
He has to make the decision of wanting a wife over a
girlfriend
When he positions himself on bended knee I will know
that he's choosing me as his queen
He will need to show me how important I am to him
I would never ever let the one thing that should be special
for me be taken away by asking for his hand in marriage
It doesn't even sound right
It's like I'm begging for him to stay with me
I rather know that he wants to stay around
By the thought out proposal from the ground
Kneel down in front of me
Make it romantic
Say "Will you marry me?
Surprise me with a wedding ring

I'll say yes
My fairy tale ending will happen that way

By: Tyra Robinson

Invitation

You and I became good friends after breaking up
Well you broke up and I was stuck
We had always kept in touch and you became my friend I
stayed in love with
You moved on and so did I with feelings still inside
When your relationship ended my relationship status had
changed
He proposed
My fiancé gave me a life I always wanted
He respected me, he never cheated…he was in love
I said yes for all those reasons and by saying yes I knew
that meant I had to stop thinking about a possible us
That was going to be hard for me to do because I had never
gave up
It was an idea I wanted to work and I needed for you to
show up
I invited you to the wedding!
I didn't expect you to come, but I wanted you there
Hoping my happy, made you care
The day came fast and before I knew it I was standing
there in my wedding dress…
Happily knowing I was going to be seeing you again
I walked down the aisle looking at my husband to be, then
I seen you there which made me smile
When I stood in front of my fiancé I seen how nervous
and how happy he was

The way he felt for me was the way I was supposed to be
feeling for what we were about to become
I was more excited inside just knowing that you were
watching me
I convinced myself if you came, you came for one
reason…to save me
The minister then said "Does anyone object to this
marriage?"
You're the person that I thought would get up and say
something but you didn't
You stayed seated and the wedding went on
He began to read his vows to me and I started crying
"happy tears"
To him my tears gave him the impression that I was
emotional about all that he was saying
I wondered if you knew my tears meant something else
because you knew me more than him
You just ruined my wedding by bringing me back into
reality
I was now officially the wife of someone who cared for me
more than you ever could
You didn't come to stop my wedding because you loved
me more than he ever would
The rest of our life together was no longer no more
All you came to do was watch…You wasn't coming to
express feelings you just didn't have anymore
You had been invited

By: Tyra Robinson

33

Wasted Time

I waited for so long for you to come back into my life
Days
Months
Years
After ten years you let me know you're ready to try again
So we met up to have dinner and talk
As you spoke you told me things I've always wanted you to
say when we were together
Hearing you say these things after time has passed doesn't
sound the same
I'm looking at you knowing that if we tried being a couple
now things would be different
It won't be those days of how we used to be and that's
what I thought we would go back to
I'm not looking at the same person I was waiting for
I'm seeing an updated version of you
I always thought when and if you did come back I would
take you back
No questions asked
It didn't even matter if I was with someone at the time
You were all I wanted, but for some reason I'm not crazy
about you anymore
Yesterday I would have said you have always been the
love of my life
Today in front of you I feel like crying because I don't feel
the same
I don't know when my feelings left

You came at the wrong time in my life
My "What if?" now had an answer
Time has changed things

By: Tyra Robinson

He wasn't him anymore

I love the way you loved me
I just don't know when it changed
You got so frustrated with things I always did, out of
nowhere those same things became a problem for you
You didn't want me to go out with my friends
You were acting jealous, but it became a little too much
You didn't like when I wasn't home at the time I said I
would be, but I said "I would be home"
At first I thought it was a little cute
You wanted me all to yourself
You were showing that you cared, but your caring ways
soon changed to me having to do what you said
You pulled me back when I wanted to leave so I stayed
just to shut you up
Argue and I was expected to listen, there was nothing else
to discuss
Your pull became a shove that led me to fall and never get
up
I never spoke up after that
Hidden marks and covering up was misleading to everyone
else
We were a power couple, but the only thing is you had all
the power and decided when I lit up
When I noticed that I should've left
I just couldn't leave you because you needed me
My body knew it wasn't ok but my mind didn't

It made me sad if you didn't feel free and I was your
freedom
I thought that if I did everything you wanted we would
just be happy with no problems
My heart was choosing to stay

By: Tyra Robinson

Family Ties

You apologized but never was sorry
Loose
I told you who she was to me
Ties
I introduced you to her because she was blood
Broken
You still went behind my back and made a fool out of me
With family
Any interaction between you and her I only let happen in
front of me, but you still found a way on your own to get
close to her
Unraveled
I didn't think you would ever do this to me, but her I
knew she never would
Trust
My favorite cousin was like a best friend to me and
because of you we are now enemies
Lies and deceit
When did you think it was ok to embarrass me?
Betray me!
It's not like it only happened one time so it wasn't a
mistake
Accidents don't happen twice
You fucked her multiple times so it was intentionally done
All the options out there and you choose my family
You chose to hurt me
I found out and you still tried to lie

It crushed me to have to go ask her why
When she covered up the story all to be with you
That's how I knew it was true
Blood isn't thicker than water
I could never have a relationship with either of you
Heavy in my thoughts
How could you be sorry when I left you and you went
after her?

By: Tyra Robinson

Dishonest

You lied
I can't stand a liar
One lie leads to another
When you tell the truth I won't be able to believe you
You can't expect me to be able to trust you again after you
told me something you knew wasn't true
I can't stand a liar
I rather know the truth
It's worse for me to find out you lied to me
I like honesty
Keep it real with me
I can't stand a liar
It creates trust issues when we never had any problems
Now I have to question everything you say to me
Your answers will take time for me to believe
It ruins a relationship
I can't stand a liar
Don't promise me anything
Promises not kept are lies too
They're called empty promises
Words that are put together that are meaningless
I can't stand a liar
A promise is the biggest lie
"I promise" sounds so promising
I don't want to hear it if you're not going to do it
There's no need to say it

Don't make it sound like a contract you signed and you're
going to abide by it
Don't share your empty thoughts
I can't stand a liar
Don't make me believe something to avoid trying to hurt
me
Don't lie to me because it sounds better than the truth
Just don't lie
Period

By: Tyra Robinson

My Heart's Racing

I'm out of breath
I'm running away from what I already know
The lies
The cheating
We been through this before and I can't breathe
Too many laps I've been running
I'm tired now
I can't keep up, you're just too much
I'm done chasing... you
I need a break
I want to know how it feels to be in your shoes
Even with set rules you still do as you please
Never caring about how much you're hurting me because
you still hear my footsteps
Do not chase me
I'm running faster because you're trying to catch up
I won't let it happen
I'm not slowing down so you could catch me
Don't chase me!
I'm running away from you and you're trying to win what
you lost
I have to gain strength if I want to end in first place
I'm focused
I can't look back because if I see you racing,
I would be seeing an illusion that you want to change once
more
It would stop me in my tracks

You're chasing me because you notice me moving forward
I don't want to run this race anymore
Do not chase me
I've won
I reached the finish line and I'm done

By: Tyra Robinson

THErapist

You were someone I could talk to
I confided in you
You were learning me and mentally taking notes
My problems, my fears, my secrets, my flaws
You knew all of me
You were my best friend
I trusted you
I never thought our friendship would end because of
everything you knew
A mutual friend
She got drunk one day and started airing out everything I
told to you, but
on top of that she let out a secret that was only meant to
be kept between you two
You kept it from me
It was about you sleeping with my man
I told you me and him were having problems after the
baby
I told you I didn't feel cute anymore because I wasn't
losing the baby weight
I told you about how he belittled me
I told you I thought he was cheating on me but then to
find out it was true and it was with you
My best friend was the one that was fucking my man!
I had to sit back and remember all that I said to you
How could you stab me in my back like that?

That crush you had on him must have never went away so
you learned when to make your move
I guess when you sat and I talked, you were just collecting
all my thoughts
You were my go to therapist, we had many sessions
Acting as if you cared about what I was saying
Listening and not displaying your plot
Now I know why you were so invested in the conversation
You wanted my life so bad that when things started going
all wrong for me, you found ways to make my man the
topic of conversation
Trying to make it as if you wanted to see if we were doing
better or still having problems so you could move in and
do everything I wasn't doing a little better
You were good at listening
You used everything I said against me
You fucked my mind up

By: Tyra Robinson

You never ended it

Let me share a little story with you
I loved a man that was never "mine"
The one he cared about before me he never lost feelings
for
I never knew that he was with me because he was trying
to get over her
I never knew too much about her or the reason for them
breaking up
What I did know is that she broke up with him
He told me he would always love her and care for her
I didn't care about that, but what he should've told me is
that he still loves her and cares for her
I was getting feelings for someone who was showing me
that he had feelings for me too
I was in a relationship getting used
I was able to figure out his password to his phone and read
through all his conversations that he had been having with
her
His ex was back in the picture making him smile
They were talking to each other almost everyday and that
wasn't ok with me
When I confronted him he told me that she was just a
friend
I didn't care about the friends he had, but he wasn't going
to have his ex around as a friend while he was with me
From what I seen in his phone they was reminiscing on
their relationship...She missed him, he missed her

They were flirting around and he was telling me he was
just playing around with her
They're were exchanging pictures back and forth and he
was trying to make me think it was ok because it wasn't an
everyday thing
It didn't matter how often or not often it happened…it
shouldn't have been happening at all
That type of friendly behavior shit was going to have to
stop if he was going to be dealing with me
He said he would stop talking to her and it seemed like for
a little bit he did
I knew he only did it because I told him if he didn't we
would be over
I knew when he started talking back to her again because I
seen a different type of happy from him
She had his heart
Unfortunately I was dealing with a heart that was in love
with someone else
He was just waiting for her to come back around when she
was ready
I had to let go of him
He was not going to let her go and I was going to have to
just figure out what to do with the feelings he did create
Moral of the story: Learn everything about a man's past
before believing you and him can have a better future

By: Tyra Robinson

She was first

There was someone before me I won't even try to compare
There were feelings before the ones you developed for me
and that I just can't compete with
Love can be felt different, and I just have to see how
different it is for me
I don't want to be stepping on anyone's feet
If you love her that has absolutely nothing to do with me
Don't involve me
Don't use me until you notice that it bothers her for you to
be with me
Opening up my heart it wouldn't be fair to me
You have got to completely be done with what you lost
and now gained with me
Love never starts with hello, you made me trust and
believe
If that's over and done, it will show and I will see
I understand love I been... in love before
You can't compete with him and I can't with her, but to
open another door you have to have an empty heart to be
filled by me, the one you opened it for
It's quite unique how love changes to not in love anymore
I will always respect the saying that "I will always have
love for you, but it's not in love anymore"
I understand it all
After all there was someone before me

By: Tinina Robinson

Torn

I'm a page away from tearing it out
We just aren't seeing eye to eye
Its like we lost our vision of what we talked about
What was so clear is now blurred with tears that keep
coming down
Falling out
I'm losing him without a doubt
Why fight if he's trying to box it out
Block it out, dip, dive and be knocked out for the count
I love him, but I'm not fighting to win his heart
Especially when he's treating mine like it's a rookie and
doesn't deserve a chance at the champion's spot
He's breaking my heart
I'm a page away from tearing it out
The lack of care
I should've been ripped it out,
But love hurts then its found are my thoughts
I just can't get past all the chapters that were already
written and that were good thus far
It was great for the start
So believable I was sure there would be no end to our book
I'm tearing up
Making words fade like ink does overtime

By: Tinina Robinson

Always and Forever

You will get a man who will tell you forever but he doesn't
mean and always
Are you listening? He will tell you always but he doesn't
mean forever
Things change
People change
Time...it's changing
The date has changed
His hours, minutes down to the second has ended
He said I will love you forever and be there always... but
he hasn't
It's not the end! I'm not dead yet but still his always didn't
mean shit
I mean forever is the day it's over when it's over and done
with
That's really what he meant
He should've said that
He should have said that the feelings would last as long as
we are together
That I love you now it doesn't mean that I will stay in love
with you forever
Words stick and he should have known better
The forever kept me, the always kept me coming back
Those words made me love him
I'm just heartbroken now that the us turned into never
again
By: Tinina Robinson

Welcome

Don't open up any doors you plan on slamming shut
My heart is trusting and it will break if it's disappointed
anymore
I believe in love, I believe in happiness
I just got a few sour apples I keep telling myself
throughout my search
Despite all the doors that have already closed, I've
managed to keep mines cracked
I don't want failed relationships to hold me back
Damage me so much that I'm damaged goods
Thinking it's my fault when it simply didn't work out
I'm telling you to not even answer if I'm knocking and you
want nothing more
Mislead me by even answering at all
It's crazy of me to want to even enter anymore...
Giving someone a chance to hurt me once more
People say let love come ring your bell because sometimes
when you're looking the same feelings are not felt
He has to want you
He has to invite you in
Opening up can be very hard... he's probably in the same
spot that you are in
Wait for the keys to jingle and somehow fit into the house
you keep locked
Even though it was never secured, it just had a guard up
wanting the security of real love
By: Tinina Robinson

* * *
51

I'm Driving

I don't think I should have to sit while you play catch up
While I was moving along you was sleeping, resting and
just not taking life serious like I was
You wasn't handling your business
Now I'm where I want to be and you're just standing up
I was in my pursuit for happiness a long time ago
You're trying to have me take a seat while you try to catch
up
I don't think so
We both had plans for a come up then the scale got tipped
and I was bumped up
It's time for you to bring your weight up, but I'm not
waiting when you had the same choices I had but didn't
take them
Where does that happen at? Just because we're together
I'm supposed to hold off to support your hustle or I'm not a
good girlfriend
While I waited and decided that being in the same place
wasn't working
Now you think I'm "acting funny"
No I just don't think I should have to sit while you play
catch up
I drove here, I didn't catch the bus and because I rode here
alone why should you come along
You have said some verbally abusive things while asking
me to sit and wait when I'm already here

People say a good partnership is helping each other on the
way
I would say yes if we started together like we were in a
race, not when I've already finished and your bell just rang
to begin
I stood up, ran and won the race
Sorry you're just too late

By: Tinina Robinson

Here's Your Closure

You need some closure, well today is it
I've fallen out of love long before you did
It's nobody's fault, it just happens then it's done
The animosity, bad blood comes from you caring more
than I ever would
I did love you more than any man I've ever loved, but the
hurt after the fact has made me hate you more than any
man I could've ever been in love with
You just never ended up the man I planned to be with
I feel I tried and tried, but you could never be him
I don't think you did enough and when you did it was
with somebody else
Funny how that happens, the fix after it's done
I made you a better man for someone else
I have my memories of the man you were
There are a lot of things done and said now from a man I
don't even feel I know anymore
Words mean nothing if they change over time and you
told me that you would love me forever
That was supposed to mean never end over time
Forever if I'm not mistaken means it will never end
You don't disrespect the ones you love especially when we
ended as friends...Hurt, I'm crushed
I thought I was secure at least in your heart
Closure now, its time to shut the book...I'll label this non-
fiction because that's what it was...Genre: Non Fiction
By: Tinina Robinson

It's Gone...The Love

His touch wasn't the same and I felt it
When he shifted in bed and moved away I felt the
disconnect
It wasn't there anymore and I knew it
I would hold it inside to not lose it
Staring too long in his eyes would prove it so I shied away
from eye contact to prevent losing him any farther
Distant I couldn't bring him any closer
I was losing sight right before my eyes and couldn't even
see an us anymore with bifocals
Blurred, tears kept me unfocused
I loved him that much that my hopes were hopeless
You can't make someone love you no matter how much
you hope for it
Wishing that he cared on every star, I wished for it
I wanted the happy back... the can't wait to see you again,
but instead I was being pushed away with no sign of loving
me back
Right before my eyes I was losing sight despite all the lacks
I acted like I didn't notice just to keep up with the act
If it was ending it was going to end I knew that, but I
wasn't going to go blind if it was hurting my feelings

By: Tinina Robinson

Faking Love

Are people really in love or just saying I love you?
It's just too easy to go on after it's done so I'm questioning every I love you and why you said it
Every relationship isn't perfect, but you try to make it...perfect
That's what love is!
That's what real love is and in love is
So a lot of people probably never really been in love, they are just saying I love you
They break up and treat the next man or woman thee exact same way that was special between you and him
How is that in love when that special occasion was replayed out over and over again?
It tells you that you were no different
If he can let me go, he can let you go too if he never talks of putting a ring on it
You're playing house up until then while giving him all you got
It doesn't work, its a dollhouse and he will get tired of playing pretend
He'll move on and find himself someone else who is ready to play make believe
It's easy for him to do because he was just saying I love you as the character you gave him who would say anything you wanted him to
He had to make it feel with you like it's the real thing between the both of you

I'm pretty sure it wasn't love though since he has moved on from you

By: Tinina Robinson

Motherfucker really

Motherfuckers really talking out the side of their neck like
they got throat cancer
I can barely hear you, but you did this to yourself
You think you choked me, but you're the one out of
breath
You said too much and now there's no going back
I was quiet when I left you alone
then I hear my name is being thrown up
What the fuck are you saying?
I didn't catch it because you're under the breath with it
Whispering with it
On some low key shit with it
Disrespectful... well disrespect you will get!
I was quiet when I left you alone now I'm all set with it
You've known me for way too long to think I was going to
sit back and put my feet way up on my throne
I've stepped down for a minute
It's not my character, but I'll entertain the clowns for a
minute
You're telling stories but not enough to be a bestseller
Your fiction is false, stop lying with it
Hurt and just don't know how to get over the shit
It shows that therapy for you might help
You're stressed and have to talk other people down to feel
some kind of wealth
I never needed you, that's a fact in itself
You're working not working for self

There's no growth in that, just a bill after bill
You're not better than, you're just dressed up and pretend
You're the perfect example of love runs thin
Where trust ends
Where friends turn enemies begins
Lovers then friend and it ends

By: Tinina Robinson

Your boyfriend or your girlfriend

The sex was mediocre, I rather the tongue
Good man, just questionable
Girly ways...Talks way too much
Cries like a baby, needs a pacifier to shut him up
I mean holds onto shit like it's stuck in his butt
Hurt to the point that lies and tea starts to spill when it
was finally done
Brewing the shit like its factory sent
It's all good to the point that it only favors him
Fuck outta here he likes milk added while he sips, his
pinky out while it tips
Talking while he drinks like he's going to get a passing
grade on a very hard test while trying to convince
That's just one of the things before even his period
Now he licks the asshole more than the puss and likes
fondle play way too much
Very, very questionable
Moaning and sticking his ass up in the air
Questionable? Legs cocked open
Ass throbbing and wet, wanting that anal g-spot touched
Questions there were way too much
Sticking his chest out, arched back...questionable?
Got me wondering who's the man because his dick only
stayed hard like a brick from the more fingers that slid in
Seriously questionable
I had to move on, let his ass figure it out
I'm kinky but still wanted a man

He went on, got a new girlfriend
He was lonely as fuck
I'm thinking girlfriends...lesbians?
Ok so move on be happy, I'm wishing them luck
Until some unfinished business pops up and I see that
there's been pillow talk
Yes it comes from the doll that is all made up, clown faced
disguised and covered up
Doesn't know me from a hole in the wall so this
motherfucker started having periods and bleeding it out
I'm assuming girly talks like girls do when they run their
mouth
She's thinking shit, hey she can believe and think what she
wants
I'm thinking he must surely take it in the ass now, shit
stinging when it comes out
Somewhere between the lines though she got me fucked
up
I'm the one who broke up
I'm the one who left
I never did a U-turn; I had simply fell out of love
She tried it flipping off at the mouth, but you learn a lot of
things from an angry person... she never better try her
luck
Moral of the poem he was never a "man"
When he love the dick more than I do...bitch please I
don't want your girlfriend

By : Tinina Robinson

Purchased man

You may have more money and a deep throat, but...
He loved me without a dime, cared for me without a
nickel and wanted me without a penny
So you see my dear real love doesn't have a price tag on it
It's not bought
Sucking him off on a lonely night is how you got him and
now he's caught...followed by the gifts of course
You caressed his ego, fucked his brain then paid your way
into his heart
It was a plot and hey if that's how you got him then he
should stay put
He was feeling neglected... you played off of that
I didn't want him so he went to second best
Him talking shit about me just shows how hurt he still
really is
Keep thinking you got him when I'm mentally in his
thoughts
He's loved me a lifetime
You're going on a couple of months
He's trying to find in you what he had in me all along
Since he's on the money train I commend him for that
You have to be happy some way, might as well have that
money intact
You just come along with the check
Signing, cashing and spending and he's what you bought

By: Tinina Robinson

He's still stuck

Bitch I'm not looking for struggling along with
I'm looking for a man that felt before being with and
settling down with anyone he would struggle to have
something
Not a life of struggling, job to job hustling
Paycheck to paycheck, bringing barely home nothing
No motivation to own something or have anything to pass
down to kids that he will leave one day alone in the world
to struggle in
No bums I need a man that's established, career first over
everything
He's broke if he's working and bringing home minimum
wage to have nothing as soon as it is cashed
Rent taking his whole paycheck
The utility bills... all late
Half ass dates to the movies and can't even go out to eat
I just can't do a broke ass man, maybe it's just me, but sex
is never that good unless you're swept off your feet
Wet I would never be
That kind of man just isn't sexy to me
Struggling along with is just not my cup of tea
I give it to you women though that think real love is
everything even if he has nothing
It just couldn't be me
My man needs to at least have something, that's real love
to me
By: Tinina Robinson

Doctor

Always the nurse, never the doctor
No financial background to pay for thee expense but even
if I had it there is no acceptance letter to let me in
Stuck in my circumstance
I had a dream one day to become more than I am
I wanted better, but nobody gave me a chance
I tried the things I was told would get me in but medical
school I was then told is a competitive place to get in
Forced to demote what I seen myself as
Get a certificate... that accepts blacks
It's still in the field just not a superior role
You're able to take blood pressure, temperature and the
weight
You're just not trusted enough to save a life or diagnose
anything
Working beneath that's how it has always been
Being told that not everyone gets in
Well is it only black women, that don't have a chance?
Just look at the stats, its one out of ten
Then look at all the nurses that are the same color as I am
We're nurses not doctors, never even considered
There should be subsidized spots to fit more of us in
We are highly educated just not all wealthy enough to
have better opportunity to not be overlooked
I want the finer things and for once something to not just
be took
I'm willing to put everything in for the career that I want

It's a privilege!
No I did all the hard work and it will never be enough
because it's just too many things that have to be bought
into and I'm not wealthy enough

By: Tinina Robinson

Your Answer Is Not Correct

You think you know but you are human just like me
You want to believe you know the answer but who gave
you the answer...
Another human that's just like you
A... human being
The studies show, the test reveal
It's just what they believe
There is no right answers
It's our thoughts and beliefs
How we've been raised and what we are taught to believe
in
I don't have to believe the same things that you believe
True and false, it's your view
How you think things are supposed to go, how they are
supposed to be
Right or wrong, who is this saying so?
A... human being
Everybody is copycats; they just go along with what's
written
People wrote it, there is no one first to say who said it
Created and designed to make you listen
People live their lives on the rules that other people made
up
History ok it happened, there are historical things and
films that show that it existed, but who made us enemies?
There are just a lot of questions that can't be answered
People are telling the story of what was told to them

Believing the answers given
It's our human error
Answering questions we haven't seen ourselves

By: Tinina Robinson

Black President

A human world has taught us that we are supposed to be
happy because we got our first black president
If there were no different, there would have been no
difference to see
I've got a black president in my lifetime probably never to
be seen again
It was historic because our history with ancestors were
made slaves because of the color of our skin
Now it reads a little different
Of course I'm proud, I don't want to take away from
something that was thought to never happen
We've got our black president for two terms to be exact
2008 to 2016 applaud that! Take a minute to embrace that
We live in a world where black lives don't matter, that's
what they say now
We were enslaved at one point
We are supposed to be ashamed of our color
That's what we are taught in every school...that you were
below us at one point
How are we supposed to get past our past when it's
brought up like it was a sport
A black president was elected to prove a point
That we are not living in a racist world
Give the black people a gift of patriotism...that should shut
them up
Black lives more than ever died under his presidency
showing that even as a leader he wasn't respected as that

No nothing changed, people can't let go because the
president elect is more like a sideshow
They made being a president a joke!
I think to discredit the one who was voted in before
The black president
This only said that anyone could be elected in
There were no runner-ups
The selection we had we were shit out of luck
I wish Michelle Obama would of run. In that we would
have got our first woman president yes black because that's
a fact but in 2020 and or if she runs it shouldn't be the
highlight over everything else
People are making it about race
I'm black and I'm proud and we should be because our race
was belittled, humiliated and tortured from the start
That also was a long time ago and
racist still exist, you just can't stop people's ignorance
There's no equal because the entire world can't come to
the conclusion that we are the human race first
Blame, blame, blame pointing fingers… you're the mistake
We are in a world where people made superior exist
Following rules in a system designed for us to listen
You're the king and queen, the police, the rich the
famous…you're the president
Be happy with what you get because we are still living in a
world where change hasn't happened yet and it never will

By: Tinina Robinson

Monitored

Who says that we are free, when we have cameras on
every street corner watching and monitoring every single
thing that we do!
Social security numbered 012-34-5678 that number in the
world that is you
We're in prison without the bars living among all the rules
Our warden is the President and Republicans and
Democrats are the guards we listen to
Freedom to breathe is taken by people with handcuffs
We can't even live in a world together without one race
feeling superior over all of us
Black lives matter!
We are still skin and color
Even the writing on the wall is documented, recorded and
kept forever
How free is it when people are put behind a wall to not be
together?
Who made up labels to segregate each other?
Who made up and gave anyone over others all this power?
Free, free, free
Why are people poor and others are living without
shelter?
How is it possible to be born the same way and above any
other?
Money holds all the power and the freedom to do
whatever

It's not the same as being free though because everyone
has to answer to someone at a higher level
America the land of the free is just a hoax and free is not
defined in the dictionary as a controlled environment

By: Tinina Robinson

I'm so glad

Gosh I'm glad I've never been raped
Raped of my innocence, my purity, my trust...
I'm glad that nobody has used me and made me feel less
than
Told me lies to get between my legs then vanish...
Hit me and tell me that I'm stupid
Verbally abusive
Feed my mind that I'm ugly and not beautiful
Made me believe that black wasn't beautiful
I'm so glad that I wasn't raped from schooling and learning
Made to believe I was privileged just because I was the
minority amongst all my white classmates
Centered out as slavery while learning that we were
actually made one of them
Words, reading, a great education, knowledge and wisdom
I'm glad
I'm glad I wasn't raped of not having a roof over my head
Of having food in the fridge
Of having money to live
I'm glad I wasn't raped of having a family the right way
When I say right way I mean me as a mom, him as a dad,
husband and wife then the baby
Bringing our baby up together in a beautiful and
wonderful environment and community
I'm glad I wasn't raped of true love with one man instead
of getting fucked over and over and over again by men I
didn't end up with

I'm glad that the ignorance in the world hasn't raped me of the good I see in each individual as a person, as a human
I'm glad nothing was taken away or forced upon me to make me feel different, to be different
I'm glad nothing has held me down, silenced me and held my mouth so that I can't breathe...shut me up or out of the world
I can't even say that I've been raped of having all the finer things in life because even that comes with a cost of no more personal space or real and genuine friends
I'm rich without even having all the money in the world
I'm healthy, I'm sane
I'm glad I'm not naked and blind to people who have been raped and understand them

By: Tinina Robinson

I showed up

Guess who appeared today...me
I sat comfortable, yes sir no sir
Doing what was expected of me
Yes, yes, yes... ok sir
Sure, no problem, I'm going now sir
Playing the part, doing my job
It's a role I applied for
Like it or not I got hired for
Absolutely sir
Being late to pick up my own kids from school, just for
him... the boss to make it home to his
I'm an employee, someone who answers to, to put food in
my fridge, to put dinner on my table
I've thought long and hard about starting my own business
Then thought about money I would be taking away from
my kids education when they are ready
The tuition and bank statements
Barely now even making
Then I thought it will be hard work and even a gamble if I
could pass the test I would be taking
I wasn't the brightest light in the box but wasn't stupid
either
I thought anything has to be better than this for my kids
for them to look up to
I appeared today and it was like I had to convince myself I
could make it

That the things that were stopping me are just challenges
and obstacles I would have to face
Nothing worth having just falls on your plate
If I wanted a better future I had to go out and get it
First step first I put my name on the start your own
business class application

By: Tinina Robinson

Dreams come true

I strive to be more than an employee
I mean who dreams about working for someone else their
whole life...Not me!
My dreams may look like they can't happen, but I'm
envisioning them for some reason
Life has a meaning and if I'm searching for my purpose,
I've already achieved them
Everyone says that a dream is a dream and that's because
they don't believe them enough to fulfill them
I'm the total opposite, I will see them
Starting somewhere I step into freedom
I want everything that I see because I've already seen them
Doors open up when you push, I'm going through them
One way or another I will get to them
Unfortunately you need to knock on doors of people who
already made it, but it's supposed to be a start to climbing a
ladder, not to just stay there
Bottom of the ladder, it's the beginning
The door opened now I'm going to start building
Meeting new people and befriending
A couple of steps up, a new position
Mastering all the skills I need, I'm in the middle
Saving and planning for the next steps I'll be taking
Looking at places I want to run my business
Made it to the top with the opening
Now it's reality, I've made it all the way up to my dreams

By: Tinina Robinson

Wouldn't it?

Wouldn't it be cool if when I laid back instead of thinking
what you could put in my mouth you really want to hear
what comes out of it?
What I'm thinking and all the knowledge
Conversations that lead into a challenge
Hours of just talking
Our minds bonding
Connecting without entering each other's body
You feel me and haven't even touched me
I'm beautiful and you haven't even seen me yet
I become naked with my inner thoughts
Letting you in is exposing myself
You fall in love with who I am
That would be cool, wouldn't it?

By: Tinina Robinson

Don't Kiss Me

Not a FAN of kissing and I'll tell you why
Oral sex isn't special between two people in love anymore
It's a routine position
Since they started eating the booty like groceries my store
has been closed and never to reopen its doors
I just love my goodies too much to let it get bump bumps
by a man who loves to go shopping downtown in every
store
I just love my mouth too much to get with a man that uses
his mouth on everybody he gets with
That's nasty and I'm just ok with never having my tongue
sucked and any sensation they say comes with it
Girls suck dick and I don't know how many you been with
and I don't want to be kissing all between who you all
have been with
For me I kiss my kids with this mouth so your dick don't
belong in it
I was done with kissing since down low men surfaced
If they want to suck dick and eat ass they should be the
ones who are open not deceiving and passing on shit that
they might catch because they're keeping secrets
Kissing is not for me since I don't know where that
mouth has been
Since he suck dick too, I just had to go back to that because
it's disgusting
To lead a girl on, have a family and kids then have
sexuality issues that you lie to yourself about

That's just crazy to me to catch a STD from someone you
thought was being faithful and not with another woman
but from another man that you haven't even laid with
I can't get passed thinking your breath must smell like shit
because you probably had ass in your face the night before
like you ate great
I'm done with kissing because it means nothing if there's
no feelings
Love and like are just two different feelings
If I were to be kissing it would definitely be because we
were in love
But, but it's just not for me because the older you get the
more you have been with and too many people your
mouth has been on

By: Tinina Robinson

In Stock

Love don't cost a thing yet I'm giving and giving and
giving...to you
Are you staying for me or for what I could do for you?
I'm so confused
You were different that's why I chose to be with you
In the beginning you acted like you wanted nothing from
me so I guess that was the proof
That you weren't using me
That everything in my pockets meant nothing at all for
you
You wasn't on the rack waiting for me to pay for you
You fell and I caught you, no register or receipt...you were
made for me and I belonged to you
Now you are the biggest price tag I have
"What can you do for me or why can't I have?"
It's all that makes you happy now, how much you can get
and brag
I'm just what comes along with the bag!
You secured me so I can finance you
I'm feeling now like I paid for you
I do everything just to keep you
Instead of just love it's "show me what you can do for me"
"Prove to me"
"I want to see how much you want to be with me"
How about if I had nothing, would you be free to me?
You're like the hidden fees that I didn't read carefully

I want to keep you, but you're just becoming too expensive
for me to keep
You're not worth the interest; I just want to be debt free

By: Tinina Robinson

Complicated

You're thinking marriage and I'm thinking this could be
complicated
The more I pushed, you pulled to keep me
You fell in love and I'm standing in the complete opposite
direction
I don't even know what I did to keep thee attraction
Love plays tricks and then it's a disaster
I rather not feel it, but you're a hopeless romantic
God!
You're thinking marriage and I'm thinking this could be
complicated
Telling you how I feel is the hard part
I wasn't trying to be misleading and never expected it to
go this far
You're a great guy, I just have a combination on my heart
and it's locked shut
Gosh why do you want to marry me, you complicated shit
You're a great guy and you put your entire heart in
Into an us and I really don't know why I can't just trust
and open up my heart again

By: Tinina Robinson

I say so

I am beautiful no matter how I look
I just don't need validation!
You telling me doesn't define that I am, that is something
that comes from within
Unfortunately an image of beautiful is what's seen first
when so many ugly people live in their image of fake
You're not supposed to fall in love with beauty; you're
supposed to fall in love with beautiful
The inner her, that's what makes her beautiful
I'm supposed to make you see me without even looking
The feeling you get when you see me, I want you to feel if
you were blind and just in my presence
Nothing needs to be said just touch, hold and squeeze me
and when you feel my feelings holding you back...that is
beautiful
When we talk and know each other's ins and outs...that is
beautiful
When it's pure, when it's real nothing is more beautiful
than that
Some people need to meet in mask first to find a beautiful
person
They are out there and they aren't the ones pointing out
their beauty or loving the attention and compliments
They are hidden behind quiet

By: Tinina Robinson

* * *
83

Self Love

I stopped caring a long time ago
People give up easy so I seen how easily they give up
They disappoint so I started relying on self
It's where I found comfort and seen I could do it alone
I got used to counting on I as one
You can't look for happiness outside of yourself
Its called loving yourself over anyone else
When you internally love who you are, you can project
better who you are
People live trying to make other people happy for them
I just live and love from afar because people will hurt and
not care how much they harmed...you
Live completely happy because your feelings matter and
you love you first
You have to care to care, so care less about what others do
Fear not losing anyone because you don't need anybody
else
Make the people in your life a want then you could
separate easily when they're gone
They're not here to stay, you die alone
There's no casket that says take who you want
We really are alone in this world so you have to learn that
you are all you got
People will say they love you then turn around and show
you how much they don't
Love hurts when you take a piece of yourself to share it
with someone and they don't care about what they got

You'll be broken in the end because you didn't love
yourself enough to stop... handing your love out
Keep it in, it's yourself love
It's yourself worth

By: Tinina Robinson

A Work of Art

I may look like a work of art
It cost a lot to be me
But still
I don't like taking pictures
I'm afraid you'll capture what I don't want you to
notice
I have to pose a certain way
I stick out my ass
I hold my stomach in
That's the "perfect body" that you see
It's all about the right angle
Tell me before you take my picture
I don't want to be fully exposed
I apply makeup to look like what you're used to seeing
I wear weaves and hair extensions
I wear contacts
That's the "beautiful" that you see
I fake smile in pictures
Sometimes I show teeth
I blow kisses
Different expressions hide how I really feel
That's the "happy" that you see
Picture perfect is what you see
I'm not beautiful though...I hide my face because being
natural doesn't work for me
I like looking a certain kind of way
I work out to keep my body fit

I try to eat right so I won't gain too much weight, but my
body is far from what I want it to look like
I'm not the right shape
I'm not happy with myself
I don't know what you see when you look at me
No matter how many compliments I get, the negatives is
all that I see
It's not even the real me
The image of myself is more ruined when anybody
criticizes me
I don't like taking pictures

By: Tyra Robinson

Face It

Makeup shouldn't make up you
It is not meant to hide your face
It's an option to accentuate your beauty, not cover who
you are… up
When you take it off people should still be able to know
it's you
Makeup should be like an accessory; you're only putting it
on to make the outfit look better
Don't put it on so that layer after layer is just hiding you
Caking it on so you can bake underneath like it's what
makes you
Makeup doesn't transform you…you do
It's meant to enhance your beauty
Lipstick, blush, eye shadow, concealer
Beautiful can't be bought
Naturally you are beautiful
If you look in the mirror and you can't see that then your
mind needs a makeover
Trying to cover up who you are is creating the look of
someone you are not
People like real things
Not something that could come right off
Looking pretty is an act if you are really not the same
when the makeup is off
"Makeup" your pretty and show off who you are

By: Tyra Robinson

Leave me alone

I rather stay in my dreams
Living in my thoughts is better than having to deal with
reality
Everyday I experience a daymare
I'm not loved by people who should love me
I'm not liked by my own peers
They bully me because they know I won't do or say
anything
They break down every piece of me that I try to fix myself,
but I'm starting to crumble
I go home to let out feelings that no one sees
I have no one to talk to
Nobody but me, myself and I know what I go through
I'm trying to fit into what everyone does but it's just not
working
I'm ready to give up…on life
I'm done hearing how ugly I am
I'm done hearing how stupid I am
I'm done listening to words that are verbally abusing me
Nobody has ever tried to get to know me, but if you ever
wanted to know a small fact about who I am, I would tell
you that it hurts to be me
Living isn't making me happy
I'm tired of being lonely
I rather sleep my life away… Rest in peace

By: Tyra Robinson

What about me?

I loved you too much because I never wanted you to think
I didn't love you enough
In the end you stopped loving me
You didn't care about me anymore
You pushed me away not realizing that you pushed me
down
I fell and the only thing I could do was get back up with
my hand over my broken heart
You looked at me with no type of sincerity
You seemed annoyed that I was trying to hold on to
something that wasn't there
This was over for you
You watched me cry
You seen how hurt I was and the comfort I was used to
receiving you didn't give to me
You handed me a tissue like the tears I wiped away wasn't
going to reappear
You wanted me to let go of the feelings I still had all
because you were investing your feelings into someone
else
She was making you happy now and because you were ok
I guess you thought I would just be ok
I didn't have time to adjust to the changes that you were
already used to
I was going to have to learn how to adjust to being alone
I was going to have to learn how to adjust to knowing that
you were going to be in a relationship with someone else

I was going to have to learn how to repair my heart as much as I could knowing that it was still going to be broken when fixed
It was still going to be holding the same feelings it always had for the same person who didn't see how much he broke it

By: Tyra Robinson

Time In A Picture

Pictures are illustrations of my life...I cherish them
I took them knowing that I captured a moment that we
can never go back to
Pictures of you and I that will last forever
It holds a time that makes me remember the way things
were
Days of my past that I never wanted to forget, I always had
my camera out and ready
I reminisce about moments of us that I can only look at
from time to time
Pictures show times of how we looked back then...I'll
never be that young again
A time when we were happy
Our first togethers...A time when we were in love
A time I'll always miss
Pictures hold onto things you would forget because you
are aging in the present and you don't remember
everything
Pictures hold stories, but it's sad because it also shows
change...a time that you could never relive
My past won't ever repeat itself
I won't ever be that age again
Last year won't happen again
I lived those moments before
Now all they are are memories

By: Tyra Robinson

Love Hurts

I was blind to things I didn't want to see
We were trying to hold on to something that we thought
was meant to be
We've been together for so long that I've never pictured
that you could be without me
I think I spent too much time with you...It led you to
cheat on me
You thought you found someone better than me even
though you weren't trying to replace me
Holding on to me was better than losing me because you
still loved me but now you cared for one
I didn't want to share you; I couldn't live like that
I gave you too many chances just to see that everything
always played out the same
I realized that repeated behavior could never change
There was no consequence because I always stayed around
to let you think it was ok
Something had to change because you can't always fix
what has been broken
When you found her, you lost me
I walked away from it all
I wanted this love to stop hurting me

By: Tyra Robinson

Master Plan

You had it all planned out
It started with making me want you
I was interested and you knew I liked you
Things progressed
You made me trust you so that I would open up to you
Things progressed
You showered me with gifts, you took me on trips
I never had a relationship like this so…
Things progressed
We fell in love with one another and everything seemed
perfect
Things progressed
You got on one knee and said "Will you marry me?" and I
replied "yes"
Things progressed
You bought a big house for us to live in, spacious enough
for us to have children
Things progressed
Aggressive behavior
Things progressed
You said you were sorry but told me that since I was your
wife I had to listen to you
Things progressed
You gave me gifts to make the apology seem more real
Things progressed
You cried so I can feel sorry for you, you cried to make me
think I did something wrong

Things progressed
I wore what you wanted me to wear when you took me
out
I ate what you made me eat
Things progressed
I had sex when you wanted to
Things progressed
You knew I didn't have family so there was no one to tell
You kept me in the house
Things progressed
You had control of me
You abused my mind to the point where I couldn't think
clearly for myself
You hit me so much that I became numb to it
Things progressed
I couldn't leave you because I was afraid
I needed you
Things progressed
I got pregnant…we had a child
Things progressed
Now I was scared because I could never leave you
Things progressed in your favor…you planned it all out for
me

By: Tyra Robinson

Trying Again

I've been single for a while, but you're making me want
something more
I'm enjoying getting to know someone else again
My heart was once closed so I didn't completely give up on
love
When you met me my heart was locked shut…I didn't
leave it unlocked to just let anybody in
You got me to open up…I'm interested
It just scares me to get so close to someone that I'm not
sure is going to stick around
I'm already used to being happy alone so now making you
apart of my life was going to be hard
A new relationship with you would mean I'm now
allowing you to make me happy in some way
This would mean that I was going to start caring about you
I was going to start growing feelings for you
It has been about six months of dating and these things
were already happening, but you wanted to make this
official
I don't want to ruin what we have now, but I also don't
want to miss out on what this could be
I've been single for so long that I'm not sure if I'm ready to
be with someone else
I'm scared of being hurt
I know that just like my past relationships this will not last
In the beginning we'll be happy for a while but that's
always how it is in the beginning

That adrenaline rush always ends and you never know
when
It's sad that I always think that starting over won't work,
but my failed relationships did this to me
The more time you're with someone the more it hurts
when you're alone again
I don't know how long we'll last, but I think I'm ready to
try
Maybe this time around things will be different and I
won't have to regret leaving the comfort zone I'm in

By: Tyra Robinson

Clueless

Why are you mad at me?
You're angry with the wrong person
Why are you mad at me?
You're showing me your wedding ring like it means
something to me
Your part time husband didn't have a ring on when he
came onto me
Why are you mad at me?
You're telling me I ruined your marriage, but I didn't
know he was married
Blame him for not caring enough about you
Why are you mad at me?
He knew when he was fucking me he had a wife at home
I thought I was laying down with a single man
I would never sleep with someone's man
Why are you mad at me?
I thought we were dating
He never mentioned you or your kids
This is all news to me
Why are you mad at me?
You can have your husband and baby father back
I wasn't taking whatever we had going on too seriously
Why are you mad at me?
He was ready to risk it all and you're mad at me
Why are you mad at me?
He kept you a secret from me and me a secret from you
I'm mad at him for not telling me the truth

Why are you mad me?
This whole situation could've been avoided if he was
happy with you
Maybe he's not completely in love with you because if he
was you wouldn't be here talking to me
Why are you mad at me?
I'm being real with you
You're really arguing with me over a man that's probably
only staying married to you because you have kids with
him
Why are you mad me?
Go take your frustration out on the man who acted single
It seems like he's ready to leave you
Why are you mad at me?
What did I do to you?
I was deceived just like you

By: Tyra Robinson

The Same

I thought this relationship was going to be different
You're starting to remind me of him
The lies sound familiar, the promises sound the same
I'm dating my ex all over again
You're starting to remind me of him
Different man, different name
You're a new character that came with the same
characteristics
I already played this game
You're starting to remind me of him
You're mask is not hiding you
Everything you're saying to me, I've heard before
"I'm sorry" is not a real apology
You're starting to remind me of him
I'm attracted to the same type...Men
You think the same
I'm hoping that you'll love me different
You're starting to remind me of him
He was everything you're becoming
The liar, the cheater
I'm used to this behavior
You're reminding me of him
Too many similarities that I can't see what's different
It's hard for me to leave because I'm hoping that you'll
change
I'm staying, waiting for you to be a better him

By: Tyra Robinson

I flipped the script

We grew apart because she played a part
Bitch the audition is over, you can have my spot
I'm not going to deal with a man that keeps secrets
Be in a whole other relationship like I wasn't enough
I must have been too much for him
You just filled in the spot for the things I wouldn't do
You practiced and rehearsed out his fantasies…something
I never would do
Now you earned your role that I gave to you because I
don't want him anymore
I hope you're happy because he didn't even want you
I guess he was trying to keep you as an extra
He had no intention of letting you shine with the few lines
he gave to you
You were living behind the scenes never being seen
You were planning on stealing my spotlight
Thinking that when I found out he was just going to
choose you and leave
Round of applause for making me laugh
He knows he just lost the star in his cast
He'll be back trying to get me back, but I'm done with his
act
I got my popcorn and soda ready to see how this plays out
Good luck on having a better ending

By: Tyra Robinson

Goodbye

You knew how to say hello but now you don't know how
to say goodbye
You left me wondering why and when I really thought
about it I cried
Minor changes became major and you was ok with it
Maybe that's when you stopped caring about me, but I
didn't want to believe it
You changed up on me
Never have I changed on you
Feelings grow but I never knew they grew up too
Yours left when they were old enough to but I guess mine
was still immature
It made me love you in a way I never loved before
I thought too much of you when you didn't think enough
of me
It was almost like you were starting to forget about me
I never wanted to become just a memory
We made so many memories
You don't know how to say goodbye because you think
you're going to hurt me
I'm already hurt
Your words is what kept me around for so long, but your
actions is what's pushing me away
Your actions are speaking loud and clear for you, it's
telling me this is your grow up moment now and I should
grow
If that's what you want all you have to do is say

It would make it a little easier for me to walk away
I'll let you go
I'll say goodbye today
Things will only get worse
I'll say it for you even if I have to say it first
If you just accept me ending it then I'll know you wanted
it to happen this way

By: Tyra Robinson

Weather Report

Forecast today: Cloudy with a chance of rain
My mind has been foggy for a couple of days
How will I know if you're ok?
My world will never be the same
I've been lost without you since you passed away
Brainstorming up ways to try to cope with this won't take
away my pain
I'll now only hear your voice by pressing play
I have videos of you that I'll get to replay
I have pictures that I'll look and stare at from day to day
All this thinking about you is causing a cloudburst to come
down my face
Funny how I predicted the emotions I would feel today
and I look outside and it's drizzling
Suddenly I hear thunder and lightning...then pouring rain
You're crying with me because you're sad in heaven today
You just hate seeing me hurting this way
Stepping outside so you can wash my tears away
It's somewhat comforting because you would do thee exact
same thing if you were standing right in front of me
Wipe my tears away
Then brighten my day as the sun tries to appear
Letting me know that we both will be ok

By: Tyra Robinson

Gas

You can go anywhere you want to go
If you can see your destination you'll get there with
determination
When you get in the driver's seat put the key in the
ignition, press your foot down on the pedal and just think
about how you took your first step...you're going
somewhere
You may get there fast or it may take some time
Just make sure you have enough fuel...you need
motivation
You don't have to let your mind race
You're not on a race course
Focus on the road you have ahead of you
You may come across other people in your lane but don't
let that distract you
Drive at your own pace
Your destination won't be easy to find because it's a place
you've never been before
Don't let obstacles and road bumps make you turn around
and go back home
No need to rush, you don't want to crash before reaching
your destination
It's only a matter of time before you'll be parking your car
realizing you drove to the right place
You went down the right road

By: Tyra Robinson

You're comfortable

I'm not asking for you to be rich, I just want you to want
more
When we met you had a job, you worked at an office
I was ok with that
You were making money for yourself
You bought me things here and there
I was cool with that
I worked as a waitress
I was making enough money to live
We were both in a good place
We were together for about two years so we thought it
was good to get a place together
Moving in was good in the beginning
We were enjoying each other
Out of nowhere the company you worked at decided it
was going to close down...that's how you lost your job
I know it's hard to find another job, but the job searching
lasted for a couple of months
During that time I decided I wanted to go to college and I
tried to get you to go too
You just didn't want to...your new job as a janitor was
enough at the time
I struggled through college with another job
You got another job too... as a cashier
We were both able to manage bills and rent
I didn't like struggling
The more education I got the more turned off I was by you

I graduated and made a career for myself as a lawyer
We both started in the same place in life but now we're in
different positions
I grew when you chose not to
Maybe I should of left you then
You look the same, you haven't changed
You got too comfortable with the way we were living
I never needed you but now I see how much I don't
It has never been about how much money you had, but
now that I'm making more, I want to live a lifestyle I can
afford
What are you bringing to the table?
All you can do is set it up
I don't want to feel like I have to support you when we
both could've been breadwinners
If you're ok with how you're living, not having any goals
in life then I can't do this anymore
I want to live better
I'm not rich, but I don't want to be with someone who is
still struggling
I'm not ok with telling people my boyfriend is a janitor
and a cashier
We aren't on the same page
We're not even in the same book anymore
I want someone who wants more out of life
Why should I have to settle when I opened myself up to
more opportunities for a better life?

By: Tyra Robinson

Before and After

I didn't fall out of love with you
I just fell out of love with the way you are now
Paralyzed from the neck down
You'll never be able to walk again
I didn't mind taking care of you before the accident
I never imagined being obligated to take care of you
It's mandatory; it's a requirement, a job now to be in this
relationship
A new role with no benefits
I wanted a life where we can take care of each other
A life where we can travel and have children
A life without you confined to a wheelchair
I didn't want this for you...for us
Your life changed but now you're stopping me from living
Everyday seems so routine now
We eat, sleep, watch tv
I push you around outside
We're not making any new memories
I feel like I'm stuck in a bad dream, but I can wake up and
leave
I'm mad at myself because if this happened to me I know
you would be there
You wouldn't see the changes, but I can't look past them
Your before and after changed so drastically
You're still beautiful, but you seem depressed every other
day
This isn't you

I'm still in love with the old you, but I don't know if I can
stay
I wasn't prepared for this

By: Tyra Robinson

Love vs Hate

I seen love, but I never felt it
She got all the attention
I got molested because I was never paid attention to
She got hugs everyday
I hugged your clothes and had to imagine it was you
She was the popular one in school
I was bullied and you never knew
She played tennis and you went to all her games
I was good at volleyball, but you never seen me play
She was beautiful
I was called ugly because I didn't look like her
She was never mistreated
I was hit and yelled at many times for no reason
She had birthdays
You never celebrated the birth of me
She was your daughter
She was your favorite
I wasn't even allowed to call you mom because I was the
daughter you hated

By: Tyra Robinson

Goodnight Mommy

A monster comes in my room at night
He's big and strong
He's very, very scary
He only comes to see me when Mommy is sleeping
I keep my night light on so I can try to hide before he
comes creeping in
The shadows of his feet appear under the door and I try to
hold back my tears
He turns off the light so I can't see him
He wants to hurt me again
Hide and seek isn't a game...he finds me
He brings me to my bed as he lies under the covers next to
me
He makes me take off all my clothes and then he touches
me
He makes me touch him too, he's very hairy
He then gets on top of me and covers my mouth
He's very rough when he's doing something inside me
When he's done he tells me not to tell Mommy
If she finds out he will hurt her and he will hurt me
I know his voice so I say "Ok Daddy"
He watches me put my clothes back on and tucks me in
like nothing happened
He leaves and goes back to Mommy's bed
I cry myself to sleep
Mommy told me monsters aren't real but one haunts me
By: Tyra Robinson

Positive

Tell what!
I'm pretty sure I know who did this to me
Actually I'm positive
Just stop telling me to call the police
Blame me
For letting this happen
I went out with my girls to have a good time
Trying to get over my ex
Let loose, stop stressing
This cute guy and I caught eyes
We went from dancing in the club to grinding in between
my sheets being carefree and not minding
Things happened so fast that I didn't realize until after,
that we just fucked without protection
I was surprised at myself … being promiscuous was unlike
me
Two months later, my physical was coming up and I
thought I'll just get cleared of this disgust
I didn't know that I would be going into the hospital and
leave out not knowing then how my life would end
The test, two weeks later
A death sentence
That guy that I met in the club murdered me
He gave me HIV
I'm ashamed because I know he's the last person I slept
with, but I didn't even know his name

I was so caught up in the moment that I let my body speak
for me
I didn't ask any questions and I didn't protect myself
I'm to blame
It's crazy that I got 100 percent on my test without
studying enough
I'll never see that man again, but I remember his face
I have to accept that I allowed this to happen so I now
have to live with the consequence
I'm an accomplice
That one night was my biggest regret

By: Tyra Robinson

Wake up

You're sleeping and I miss you when you are
I'll let you sleep but please wake up for me
It's the only time you leave me
I always wake up before you so time that passes as you
sleep is when I'm alone
I'm jealous of the night because you sleep so peacefully
I don't think that you will wake up
It's the only thing that takes you away from me
You're resting, but I feel alone
You go to sleep before me
I wonder if I'm in your dreams
I hold you close to pretend like you never left
I lay on your chest just to listen to your heartbeat and
eventually I go to sleep missing you as if you are going to
stay gone
I feel like I lose you even though you're there
My dreams keep me occupied then
I'll let you sleep
Just please wake up for me
In the morning I have a hard time leaving you alone
I end up waking you up just so you won't sleep the day
away and to bring some comfort to me
When you get up I feel more awake
Our days go by so fast, but I enjoy every minute with you
I'm only reminded of the time when it starts getting dark
Only then I know the night will soon be stealing you again

It's the only time you leave me even though I know it's
temporary
If you make sure you wake up tomorrow and the next day
I'll let you sleep as long as you wake for me each and
everyday
You leave me but you always wake up never leaving me
here alone
I wouldn't want to sleep without you
It's just the only time you leave so I fear losing you

By: Tyra Robinson

Past Life

I don't know you
I fell in love with the part of you I knew
I didn't know there was so much more to you
Your past is a big part of who you are and that's the part of
you I wish I knew before falling for you
You never talked about your childhood
You didn't want me to meet your family
I had guessed it was because you had grown up and
wanted to leave your past in the past
The closest person to you is your best friend
He grew up with you
He told me everything I wanted to know about you
He's the reason I now understand you, but it made me
scared of you
You were molested by your brother
You don't talk to your mother because you told her and
she didn't want to believe or help you
You seen your father die when your sister killed him
A lot has happened to you
At school you hung out with friends who got you into
stealing and doing drugs because it was cool to them
You dropped out and was homeless for a while until you
and your friend decided to change your life for the better
Who are you?
Now I'm here regretting hearing everything you kept from
me

You had all these issues growing up and I didn't know who
I was dealing with
I don't want to stay with someone who's been through so
much
You might have built up anger and snap one day and I was
clueless to what for
I would be explaining who I knew you as
I didn't know what you dealt with and I don't want this
anymore
I wouldn't want our children to be related to so much that
has happened in your past
I don't want to stay with someone that needs therapy
Something has to be wrong with you
Hiding your past when you clearly need to talk
Maybe it's something you're trying to forget but it's
something you lived
It's never going away
This is who you are

By: Tyra Robinson

Life

Before I knew you I loved you
When we met I fell in love with you
You became my everything in seconds
I never knew a big change in my life could come from
someone so small
You changed me
I had someone to live for
You gave me a new meaning to life
I had to teach you things even though you were teaching
me
I learned how to become a mother without any written
instructions
I got to witness all your first
I seen new changes in you everyday
Crawling became walking
Crying eventually faded away
You went from drinking bottles to holding your own sippy
cup
You went from not being able to say anything to talking
away about everything
You became more and more independent even though you
still needed me
Time allowed you to grow up so quickly and I've been
there to watch all your phases
Physically you're appearance was changing but mentally
all I seen was my little baby still staring at me

I never thought I would be so scared about letting you
grow up
The time was coming where I would have to let you go
Without you holding my hand, I wasn't ready to watch
you walk off alone
I wanted to always be around to protect you
I wanted to make sure you didn't get lost
I wanted to make sure you got to class, but I had to realize
you wasn't a child anymore
I had to learn to be there for you from afar
I would have to distance myself just enough so you could
do things on your own but know that I'm never too far
You wanted to leave me to go to college
It was your way of saying I'm ready to try to live on my
own
I had to prepare myself for the day that you would come
back to me as an adult

By: Tyra Robinson

Love and In Love

Option 1) Sometimes happiness ends in heartbreak
Option 2) Sometimes heartbreak happens before you find happiness
We don't get to choose
I experienced heartbreak first
Life decided for me how it would play out
I dealt with my ex for so long thinking he would change
I was in love with him thinking he was the "one"
He lied, cheated while I stayed faithful
I wanted us to last and work
The only reason it ended was because he didn't respect me anymore
He kept doing what he wanted to do not caring that we were in a relationship
I had to end it
It ended in heartbreak because he never tried to fight for me
He just let it go and moved on
I thought it was love
The only good thing that came out of us being together was our kids
I didn't want to rush into anything new with someone else
My kids were everything...being single worked for me
I was content and happy with myself, but when happiness came along it was something I wasn't used to
I wasn't used to someone wanting to listen to me
Someone giving me all of their attention

Someone wanting me
He accepted my kids and showed me what real love is
It was hard to trust him, but he never gave me a reason to
not trust him
I didn't know I would find the true meaning of perfect
He treated me how I should've been treated in the past
This felt right
He even asked me to be his wife
My in love found me after heartbreak
I think happiness is meant to happen that way

By: Tyra Robinson

You and I

Love becomes a story to tell...it last forever
It's an everyday movie we live...it's never ending
People watch us and can see how much we love each other
It's real
I know I'm in love because my heart is
I fell as soon as I seen you fall
I lost my heart to you
The start of us was something special
You had your mind set on getting me even though I
pushed you away
It was so cute to me that you never gave up
Even though we're together you're still chasing me
You appreciate me
You chose me in a world full of choices
I can't believe men like you still exist
You're my dream in reality
I'm in love because I love you
I look at you and know that you're the one
My life wouldn't be the same without you
I couldn't even imagine it
I would be more than alone because you are my life
I miss you when you're with me
Our bond is so strong that I know the rest of my life will
be with you
There's no doubt about that
I'm never letting you go and you'll never let go until
heaven takes you away from me

Even then I'll still be loving you
Real love never changes

By: Tyra Robinson

Play our song

Here we are just you and I but it feels like someone's
watching
Standing face to face...
I place my hand in your hand as you place your arm
around my waist
We take our first step to the right and then together we
move to the left
We start off slow as our bodies start to connect
Our bodies begin to sway from side to side as we hold each
other close
I lay my head on your chest realizing that we are now
both moving to the beat of the same song
A song that I had been waiting to dance to with you for so
long
You now feel the rhythm my heart has been dancing to,
you hear our song
Now we are in sync as our bodies grind
I look up and stare into your eyes
Our bodies disconnect
You begin to spin me around
I'm in total bliss
I never danced with someone before like this
One more spin and then you pulled me in close just before
you let me go
I guess the song was over for you but it's still playing in my
heart

The onlooker caught your attention and you left me to
watch
When you're done dancing with her, I'll be ready to dance
again

By: Tyra Robinson

Gone now

Someone who said that they would love me forever loves
me no more
I looked back and the promises were all destroyed
Questioned if they even were meant when he said them
I'd wondered if thee emotional attachment meant
anything to him
Physical touch, was it just sex?
Questioning everything since he up and then went
I figure he was gone long before he left
I didn't know how to take that
You said that you would love me forever
You said that!
Angry now that his words were fake and made up
I believed nothing after that
I just couldn't do that...to myself
Open my heart and have it torn out
Breathing off of every word like it was giving me life just
to feel that
Love me forever? Why did I even believe that?
Forever will only last in the dictionary as a definition
I had to learn that for myself
I took a step back and let him walk out my life so I could
love me before I could love anybody else

By: Tinina Robinson

A Ring

I don't want to sleep with you
I don't have the proposal or the ring
I mean what would make you think that you did
something that special
Enough for me...to open my legs
Taking me on dates and treating me with respect
Respecting me would be putting a ring on it first
A legal commitment and expecting nothing more before
that
Am I not worth that?
I mean making love should mean that you are in love with
I don't just open my legs to get fucked, to get off then be
fucked over and left
What kind of woman do you think you are dealing with?
Dating but never the marriage?
Years and years together with no real commitment
The ring is the only way in
It says I see bigger things than just spreading your legs
Loving me was never about that
You treasured me enough to want more with a ring

By: Tinina Robinson

Wait In Line

If you're giving it all to him, what is he waiting for?
It's like walking to the front of a line in a restaurant
without calling and everything you want being prepared,
ready and handed to you
Wait
There is nothing to wait for, that's why he leaves
What would he have to wait around for?
You're already feeding him entrees and he didn't even ask
for it while seeking his attention...at the door
Never making him have to chase, just samples shoved in
his face and he questions if he wants to eat there at all
I get it you're a new place... strategy it takes but aggressive
with a new customer sometimes makes them walk right on
by
It could be a big mistake
They won't eat what they don't have the taste for .
So no matter how much you toss it in their face, it's not
looking good to them
Try being the special dish
The one advertised that's very expensive, but worth every
penny if they get

By: Tinina Robinson

Men Hurt Different

When a man is hurt by a woman that he really loves, the
hurt carries on
He doesn't open up and love again
He blames everyone then after for his bad judgment
He acts like love doesn't really exist
Hurt he has succumb to it
Why is it ok for a woman to get over it but not a man?
I'm just not sure why a woman gets over and moves
through it, but a guy hurt screws with every other woman
he comes in contact with
Why does it break his heart instead of mold it...
Makes it stronger to love the next girl with
Men make it like love never hurt anyone but them
Is it because he trusted and handed her his heart and acted
like feelings couldn't change on her part?
Does he think because now that his feelings are invested
that she should know this and never break it?
Settle and there be no escape route
Love hurts and if it ends the next person you have
relations with shouldn't get screwed because someone else
couldn't love you like they could
You men that do this need to understand to close one door
before you blame the new one you open
Not opening it completely and acting like you aren't still
hurt causes problems in the beginning of a new start

By: Tinina Robinson

Boyfriend or Man?

Are you my boyfriend or are you my man because you
keep doing boyfriend shit
I don't need someone that says he's mine and keeps being a
boy friend to every other bitch that wants... him
My man, a man would end friendships that could
jeopardize our relationship
He would pick and choose what's more important
Put that to bed... put that to rest
Let anybody know that's trying to mess up our bubble of
happiness that you would dead that and end it
Instead you're acting like a boy that just got his first piece
of pussy and your dick is hard on Viagra and keeping a stiff
It's standing at attention for all these women that pay
attention
Little boy shit just not on your grown man shit yet
Where is the respect that I'm supposed to get? Making the
relationship that we have separate and different
If I'm treated the same then how am I supposed to feel the
difference?
I want a friendship from the boy that became a man that
doesn't still act like one...Look me in the eyes and tell me
I'm the only one and that shows
Choose a future with instead of being with temporary hoes
Knows my worth, selects me first
Boy or man, this I need to know because I need to be with
a man and not a little boy anymore
By: Tinina Robinson

Fairy tales

I'm the one who fed you a story and never turned the
pages
I intended to do all that I said
I just couldn't write it into existence
You're a queen, I wrote it right there
I just wasn't the king to put the crown on your head
I promised a ring, the house on a hill
A dream
I did love you but feelings change
I've wasted your time while you were waiting for the
chapter to change
It was a string, a puppet, a play
A character you wanted
You know the knight in shining armor, they don't really
exist
I made that character up so that you can believe in
something
I entered your story not wanting the same things
I should have never said all that I've said but you were
eating it up
We do have some memories written, I just can't finish the
book
I want you to turn the page and get everything you
deserve
I wish you didn't believe in fairy tales

By: Tinina Robinson

Pinocchio

Lie after lie
Your nose is growing
I don't even think you know when you're telling a story
It just became so natural to you
I see your nose...growing
String after string...I'm pulling
Tugging and grabbing
Are you really without... feelings?
Your showing, your nose...I see it growing
I just want some real...emotions
So upset that your nose is touching the ceiling
My tears are... overflowing
Scared to ask another question, you might start performing
One lie after the other...until you're
Unrecognizable
I thought only fictional characters existed in fairy tales,
but you're real, and lying right here beside me
Do you feel anything, while you lie to me!
Yes as you turn and poke and almost blinded me with the
new growth of the lie you just told
I can't even tell when it's genuine anymore
Fuck outta here...you're lying again

By: Tinina Robinson

Mirror

It's like I'm seeing myself in the mirror for the first time
because I haven't looked in a while
Unconcerned with what everyone thought, I didn't have
to look and check myself
Didn't care what the image looked like, I knew how I felt
Confidence runs deep
It's in my bloodline, mind, body and self wealth
Yet I looked because too many people were looking and
with their eyes, they spoke
With their expression, they choked and their body
language they moved away, tightened up and with no
sound laughed and laughed hard like I was a joke
I looked because its people who make you insecure!
So I stood there and I stared very hard at myself and still
didn't see nothing really wrong but a few pounds that
could be dealt with
Still beautiful but now my mind I had to fix
This never bothered me before until wandering eyes of no
one, of people who don't matter said that it was just ugly
and needed to be fixed to fit in

By: Tinina Robinson

Black Men

Why are so many of our black men in prison?
Aside from "they" are just out to get us
Are you bad or just have bad in ya?
I think none of the above
For some, it's just in you to take care of fam and without a
job fast money is appealing
Struggling from nine to five to not have a penny left ain't
what's up
No real way to come up
Your family not having enough and you feel less than a
man because you can't help
Prison with the choices you make because that's the only
way you can live and be ok
If the government got the tax of it, I don't think they
would really care what you did
Same with prostitutes selling their own body
It's their money, but the constitution wants to have the
commission
Educated but still stealing
Ruining their lives before they are even men
"Selling" to crackheads that are on drugs and out there
getting but legalize it, get a copay, how is that different?
No clothes to wear to school, everyone clowning you
Sneakers with some silly and fucked up name
Now you have to sit in class and feel ashamed
Globe Santa, no real Christmas
I don't blame my mother... it's the system

I would never blame her for not being able to meet the
demands of today's living
Single mother, the only one caring, she gave me
everything
Would skip a meal to not take anything away from us
A parent forced to work overtime instead of parenting
It puts on pressure, forces these young men to live before
they have even lived
Who doesn't want to be living comfortably, lighten the
weight of the only person they see struggling
Work
The only jobs they give us is minimum wage, forcing us to
be on the streets... some even with a degree
Open up better doors and I am sure you would see better
outcomes instead of the cell to all these black men in
prison

By: Tinina Robinson

Karma

Let's be clear I didn't break his heart, I crushed his heart
He hurt me and named me Karma
So I did what would break him in two
I did some shit I said I would never do
Even wasn't going to be fair when I divided
When we part ways it won't be equal hearted
He left me without a heart and I left him with one to fix
He would need to put all his pieces back in
Revenge sex can hurt like hell, but it's ten times worse
when it's with your best friend…Double revenge
You see I always knew his friend had a thing; I just never
acted on it out of respect for him
Feeling disrespected I let it slip in but it wouldn't count if
he didn't know I spread my legs for him
I made the bed, laid in it and made sure that he would
come in...
to find me with my legs up and his friend between them
Lights on, I held him in as soon as I seen my man watching
while he stroked it in
Looking right at him I said "harder" to his friend
"Fuck me" as he moaned it in
So into me he didn't even see my man standing there
I said to them both "how does it feel"
Crushed my man's heart while his friend was falling in
love
Held the condom up and said "I told him to take it off"
By: Tinina Robinson

Recording

Playback
Rewind...it didn't just appear
My attitude towards you grew over you not being there
From the lies you told, it made me not care
While I'm being faithful and true, you were doing you
What was I supposed to do?
Move forward
As I did after listening to it all and it not making sense
Rewinding it back, the song started to skip
It started repeating the same shit until I got tired of
hearing the same lyrics
Changing the song up, I'm rapping like Twista
You had to catch the words that I was spitting
Everything was pouring out but it was fast
You couldn't comprehend all that I was saying
You fucked up, that was all that I was saying and now the
playback button has been hit and I'm playing
Broken record, you lost me when it stopped working
I'm listening to all types of music in all types of languages
He's Latino but I'm dancing and whining on reggae
Salsa, I'm learning to do the merengue
I'm just open to live music
Maybe one of these songs will open up feelings but right
now I'm just listening

By: Tinina Robinson

Trust is an issue

I'm not a trusting person so your actions are the only
words that will speak to me
Say it again!
You have not done what you have said yet to make me
believe what you are saying
Pain is a mistake most people let happen
By putting so much trust in someone else for their
happiness
For me trust is not in the vocabulary
I've heard things and seen different to make me question
everything thereafter it's said
You could be hurt real, real bad with empty promises
My pinkies never crossed to be broken apart, I swear
Letting someone have that much control, you let your
own power go
You're hurt, disappointed then opened again for another
lie to be told
Breaking you down bit by bit
That's most women who listen to lies and think they can
be fixed
What's done is done, now the broken parts won't stick
If you have said it to me, I expect it to be done exactly how
it was said
I won't listen then after if your word is not kept
Pain is only felt when you care too much so letting
someone in is already trusting too much
I'm in love with my expectations being met

You could just call that in love with self and trusting no
one else

By: Tinina Robinson

Lesson learnt

Pain has entered once and I've learned my lesson
I've got my master's degree in the hatred of men
Disappointment, I'm going to teach women that nothing is
sacred
Open your heart and it will be taken
A man has stepped on mine... buried it in sand
Then it washed away like I never had one to begin with
In an ocean of tears I was drowning in them
I will never open my heart again now that I found out it
was treasure
It was worth too much for someone to get their hands on
in the first place
Locked away, people mistake me for heartless
If a man looks my way, he better pretend he's blindly
staring
I'm not nice, not flattering
I'm like security protecting something you could never
have now
There's a bulletproof glass up
It will never shatter again
I've learned and the pain is just too much to go down that
road again

By: Tinina Robinson

DNA, Not Dad

You're a father to who estranged father! Deadbeat father!
How do you expect me to respect you when you never
were there?
Solely off of the title of you making me but never being a
dad
What part of the DNA says that it's ok to make but not
raise a child that you helped make?
I'm sure it's not 99.999 percent
You still want recognition and to be loved like a father
who took care
Well love is developed; it's not just a natural trait because
the bloodline is there
This is on you, you pushed me away
That builds bridges, that creates hate but yet after we are
adults we have to excuse the behavior
No! It's not ok
You made me feel like a mistake
Your actions spoke volumes and it was loud and clear that
I wasn't important enough in your plans to stay
When you ended thee relationship with my mother, you
didn't have to end one with me
You laid down comfortably all these years knowing that a
woman played your man part and you slept like a baby
She did well by the way, can't you tell
You have nobody to blame but yourself

By: Tinina Robinson

Daughter

Girl do you feel more or less than a woman since you took
the man that was supposed to show his daughter how to be
treated from a man from him?
He showed her there are no good men...including him
She was supposed to learn that from him!
He left her and never returned
Are you proud you're who he left her for?
Even a call is a force
Where is the encouragement on their relationship?
Are you that important?
You're happy while their bond is broken
How do you turn your back on the first lady in your life
over a bitch?
I'm talking to him!
I will never understand it, I just don't get it
She's supposed to be his princess, a queen in every sense to
him
Daddy's little girl, well he got you that he sleeps with and
he's so comfortable that his "head" hasn't come out of the
clouds yet...He's in heaven so he made his daughter dead
to him
His presence doesn't have to be with you present
If the requirement was without you there then you should
have let him go
There was nothing or nobody who could take her place
then along came you, to make her feel less important
Hurt feelings, he didn't care for them!

As long as he was laid up with you, he forgot about the
one person in this world who thought the world of him
How do you sleep comfortable at night not knowing if
your daughter is trying to find outside comfort?
I'm talking to him!
Believing that anybody that shows some kind of love is in
love with her
He don't give a fuck about her, but she's ok with being
mistreated because her dad has done it to her
She accepts disappointment so well; it's all that she knows
This man doesn't love her, but her dad showed her how
much so a man won't
How selfish can a man be raising a daughter in this world
to not be there for her to show her to love herself first?
My question stands, do you feel more or less than a woman
that my daughter feels her dad doesn't love her because of
you who he chose over her?

By: Tinina Robinson

My biggest accomplishment

Pride never sat so well on my shelf
You see one life we live and I don't want unspoken words
to haunt anyone I never said them to
Just one life we are given, and we can't miss sorry if it is
never felt
I'm sorry even if it isn't my fault
Who's right and who's wrong, who cares... that time is
gone
I promise I meant nothing that came out my mouth
I was angry when I said it, and I wanted you to hurt
because I was hurt
I know all my feelings came out but look at pride when
you put it up... the puzzle gets fixed, before an empty
piece is missing then it's left undone
I apologize, I forgive... they are just words to accept or
dismiss
Pride then hate and anger could start to build when all it
takes is a conversation to fix
Wasted time didn't need to waste
Building memories could have been taking place
I'm only here once
I'm trying not to make any mistakes
Love happy, be happy and take a breath in each blessing
we are able to take
I have a place for pride, way up on the top shelf
I climbed up and put it up there myself
I don't want the loss before you have left

Looking up and telling the world how I felt
I don't want you to live in songs remembering sad things
The shelves are where you put all thee important things
The things you are proud of the most and pride is at the
very top of them

By: Tinina Robinson

You've failed

Sweetheart all you are is a cutie pie
When we met everything was done to please me, now you
say things that are never done!
F's across the board for effort and completion
I told you from the start that the worst thing you could do
to me is say something and don't mean it
Excuses, I don't need them
I've been disappointed, let down too much to accept them
If you tell me something I expect them
You've failed!
Erase every answer to all my questions
You were a tester and now I have to start all over with the
next guy
A whole new test and you're stepping up like you studied
hard for this makeup
I don't want you to answer how I want you to, only honest
answers that you won't make a mistake on
Don't answer to pass the test, be 100 on your answers
I've took note of all your effort, coming back to get your
grade up
Disappointment is never the answer so if you say
something, do it and you will get an A+
There won't be another retake
Begin again, it's timed and they all must be filled... in

By: Tinina Robinson

I'm not the same

Invested time is supposed to say that I was different
Sure we moved on but you don't treat me differently
Understanding things in life change but we have history
We have changed, but it didn't change the chemistry
Respect is what you give to me
If it was real love, true love... those feelings you will
always have for me
Some things end to keep what we have between one
another
Sometimes that's the only way that the love won't die with
each other
You don't share a part of your life to say that that part of
life wasn't a piece that we didn't have together
It was a part together that just fell apart and we weren't
able to stay together
We were together
It will always hurt that it ended, but I don't want to lose a
friend in you because the title isn't boyfriend or girlfriend
I think that is why so many people rather keep the
friendship because you lose both after it ends when it's a
relationship

By: Tinina Robinson

Compared To

First love, all I can say is she wasn't me
She was the first to make you feel, to make you smile
To make you happy and fall in love
It was her who got to see your pure innocence
The shyness when you touch
The grin instead of you laughing it out
Catching you staring then pretending like you wasn't
when she looked
Calling and being scared to say what you want
She was someone who made you blush then try to act like
you didn't like her even that much
At one time she was all you could think about
Someone you had a crush on, who got your first kiss
Sleepless and restless nights
Someone who you would lay up all night and think about
Anticipating seeing the next day, you would stay awake
You would stay up
You learned to love and it started with her
First love is first place because there was no one before...
her
They're a special person because they hold a first
I could be jealous but what for
Everybody has a first that they lost and had to learn their
first heartbreak from
I wasn't the first but I wish I was in so many ways but
more so to say I opened the door because everybody is
next to who stood in that place after her

By: Tinina Robinson

148

Doll

Always happy nothing can frown this made up smile
I'm not allowed to cry so tears you will never see run
down these cheeks
I mean mess my mascara up...for what!
Flawed, not as far as you can see
When you look at me you have never seen someone so
well put together, based off of looks
That's how I appear to be
Look behind this beautiful face, it's broken underneath
Scrapped and scarred...not complete
I'm a trophy for someone who's insecure, to hold up and
say look at me
Dressed in the highest fashion, hiding behind pretty
Idolized because I look perfect
Flawed never looked so good, you can't even tell it's not
me
Don't you just love my shoes?
I own them in every color and in every brand
It's a distraction from a possible bruise that was missed...
aren't they cute?
My mansion is more like dreamland
It has everything in it to keep me put and to keep my
mouth shut
A dollhouse off on an excluded piece of land
It's where he can do what he wants and nobody will hear
When we appear again I will be back made to strut, marks
covered up and a doll that will never speak out

By: Tinina Robinson

Lonely Star

Lonely star you are the brightest
Among all the stars you shine brighter
You think nobody sees you
Even though you're the shooting star
The lucky one up in the sky
Looked at and wished upon
You don't feel like anybody sees you at all
It's the star that they are looking at
They see a dream they wish they were like
It's not so bright in the daylight
For you don't want to be seen so much as a starlight
When there is no stage, you're still human
When there are no eyes watching and dreaming
All you want is to be seen first then noticed
You are human, you are a person
Stardom is an illusion
Making it appear that you are too far and untouchable
You're not up in the sky; you're down here with us
Let the stars be known for what they are
I still see you shining, just not up in the sky
I still see you as the birth name you were given
You thought that nobody was paying attention
You just want to be treated as a human because that's what
you are
People forget that because they see you shining but
putting you on a pedestal isn't helping
Making people fans and you wealthy

Then you forget we are the ones who helped you get there
I can understand the loneliness
You have nobody you could trust
Paid for friends, nobody who knows who you really are
So I guess lonely comes with the job
Even though you're idolized by the world

By: Tinina Robinson

Touch me where my spot...starts

Touch me where my spot...starts
In my thoughts, in my mind is where it begins before I can
even get hot
Stimulate conversation
Intelligent ones
Show me just how smart you are
Show me how curious you really are
I'm not a quick study, I'm just not
So you will have to show me how interesting I am as your
studying to learn what I'm about
My inside and out
Take notes to pass without mistakes
My likes and dislikes should be very important in your
intake...
It will count as a grade
If you're really paying attention
That's the turn on that's touching my... g-spot
Seeing how into me you really are
I can release better when we do touch because if you
passed with flying colors... I opened up
You're interested, and we're not just fucking, but we're
making love
The touch isn't lust
The pumps aren't just for a nut
I'm hot and wet
You want me to orgasm before you cum
Whispering what I want

Saying my name because you know that's something I love
A+, that's what you get, an A+ for falling in love

By: Tinina Robinson

Bitch Where?

You have got me confused with a female that is a dog
Running around and listening to every bark that barks at
her
Ready to back that thing up, and let him slide right up... in
her
Excited because he growled then sniffed it out
Falls right into position with just thee approach
Calling me a BITCH, let's be very careful with that word
that you chose
That girl, she is known in every house and around the
block
In every conversation as a thot
Tell me one dog that gets around that has ever had my
name in his bark
Let's be selective with your words because bitch is in no
way in reference to me and should never be used
Description, it's usually on all fours
Sucking a dick or getting that back blown out
Holding tight onto that collar because her leash came
off...doggy style
She's the one you'll find in the dog pound
Never chosen because she got rabies or some other shit
She thinks she's a bad bitch because of all the attention
that she gets
Let's number it:

#1 She knows she's a bitch
#2 She's nothing to chase
#3 Her nametag is all over the streets
I'm just none of the three; you have got me confused with
a female that is a bitch

By: Tinina Robinson

You only live once

We have one life and we live in one world
That's it!
People have complicated shit
Any other color than white there's hate against
A race
It has divided us all
People felt someone, one had to play leader to us all
Who has disconnected the world so much?
We are the only ones here so I would have to say people
That's my answer to it all
There's not a superhuman that lives on the earth, it's a
made up character who saves the world
All the problems out there, we have created them all
I'm still wondering why the world isn't smart enough to
figure it out
You make a future to better the odds but if we are not all
even the scale tips and the equation is all off
Why do people not care about people?
That's the question to it all!
We are stuck in the same place, yet there are humans that
are poor
There are humans without food, without water and even
shelter amongst all of us
Money is made from machines so why isn't it helping at all
Especially when you are paying talented people who use
their talent to perform for us all

Rich, they decided to show it off, but the underdogs are
the people working at regular jobs
Struggling to have nothing at all then won't be noticed at
the end of it all

By: Tinina Robinson

Let The Grip Go

Men will tell you "I love you" under pressure
When they see that your feelings are too invested
You're crying and shit just because he left you
So I love you follows for comfort to let you know he cares
but it's not love yet
I love you, I love you, I love it
While you are fucking
The pussy is good, it's something his dick hasn't felt yet
It's warm like chocolate when it melts, and it's put in so he
can't get the taste out his mouth and he loves... it
He would say anything even spell it
I love you, I love you, I l o v e... it
He's in love with the pussy that has whipped him
Baby girl that's not in love with
He prefers the pussy over you so I love you is said so you
stay wet...Men will tell you "I love you" under pressure
Now when he cares, and he really does, and he sees that
there could be something
You're suggesting marriage, the ring, and baby carriage
He's feeling under pressure to not lose you because he does
see the potential
You're threatening to leave so I LOVE YOU with every
emotion is said without a doubt that it's just not that yet
It's to make you stay, to keep you
He wants it to be love but sometimes while it's happening
you stop it with the squeeze you put on him
By: Tinina Robinson

Be careful what you say to me, my heart is listening
– Tyra Robinson

Other Books by: Tinina Robinson

ISBN-13: 978-1514125915

Poetry at its best about people's lives fitting in their own shoe size

Type in You Don't WALK In My Shoes on Amazon to get your own copy

ISBN-13: 978-1530014965
ISBN-10: 1530014964

Available on Amazon

Don't just read this...go to Amazon and write a review right away before you forget. Thanks

Made in the USA
Lexington, KY
18 April 2018